Horses
Coloring Boook for Adults 2

Sophia Payne

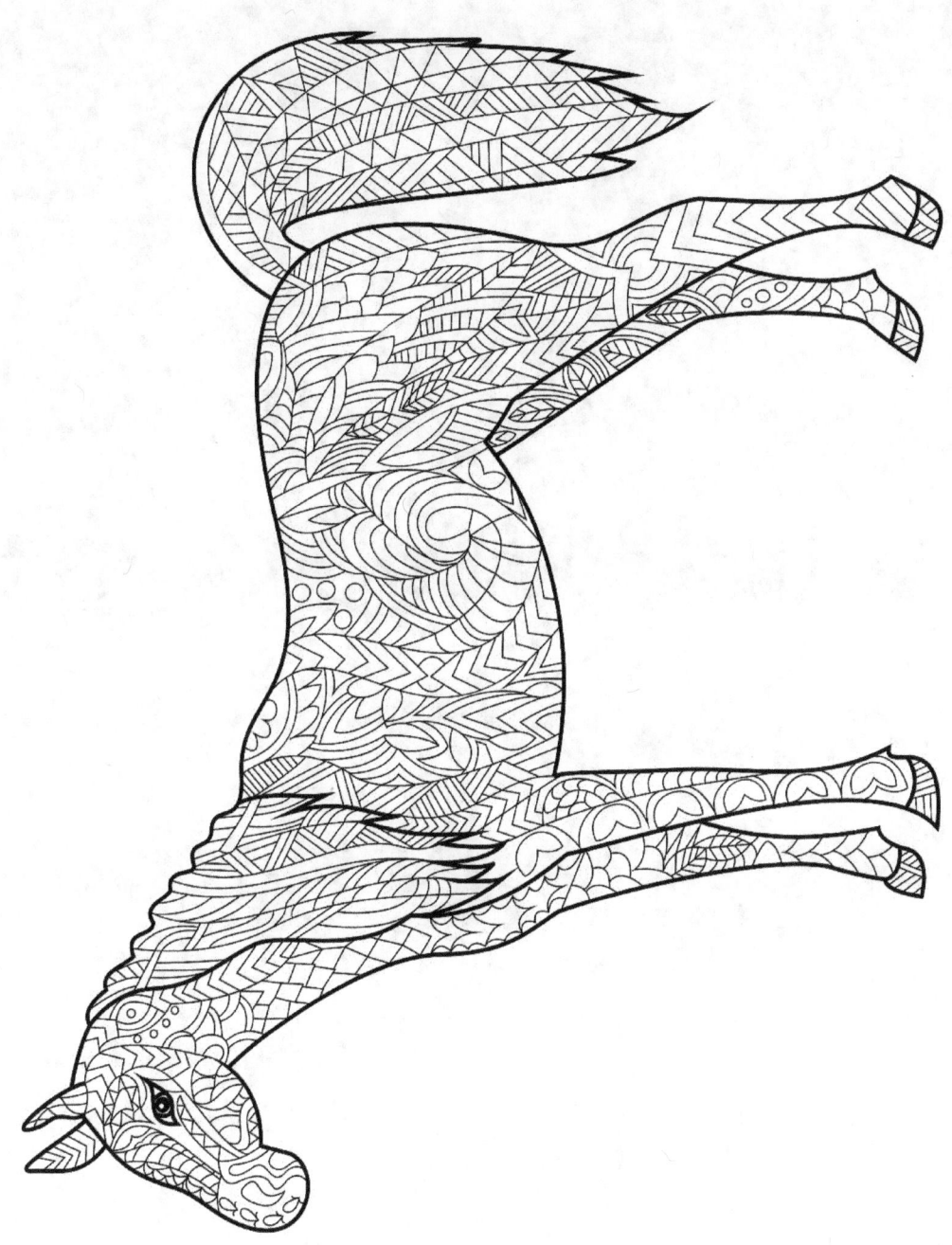

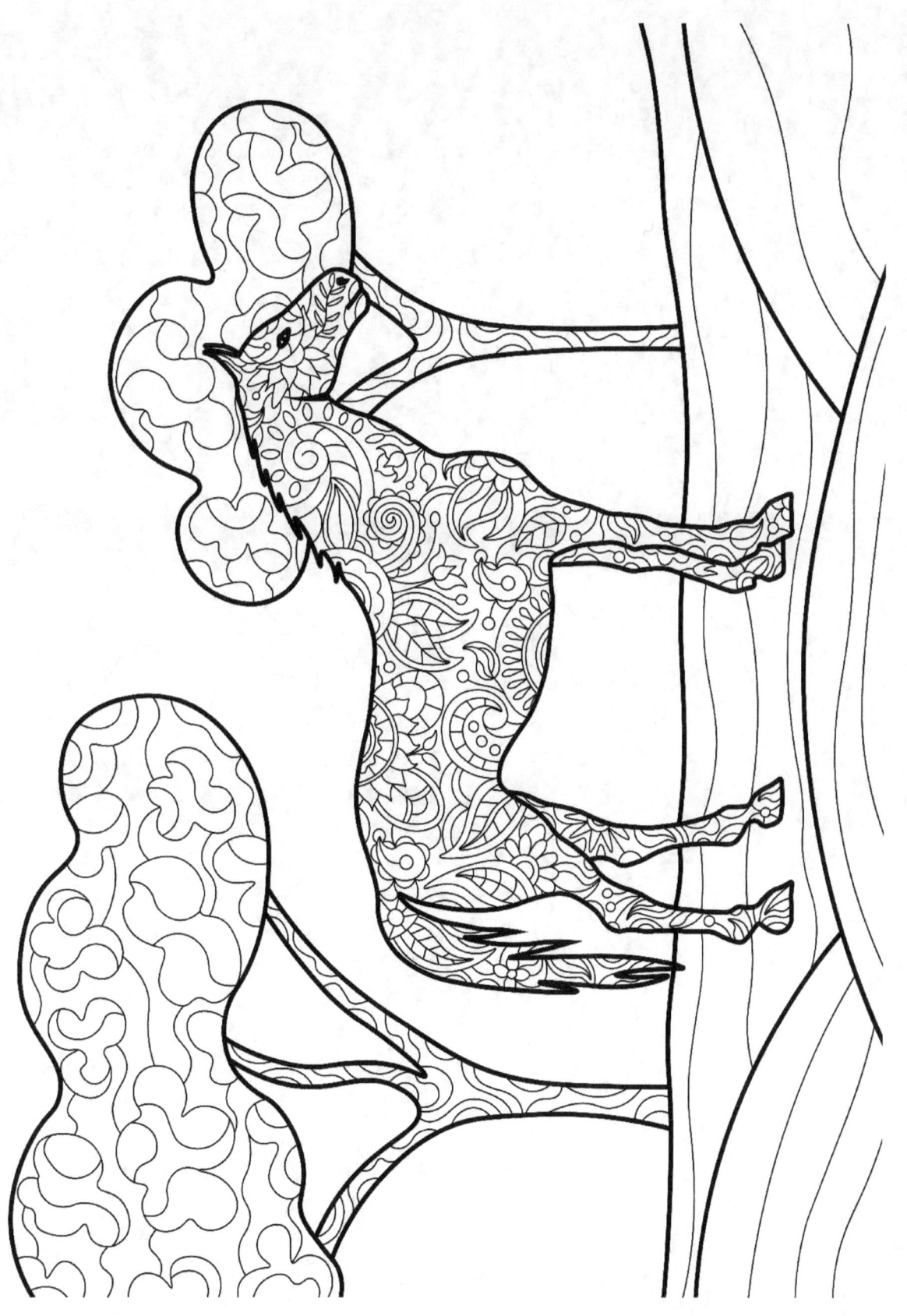

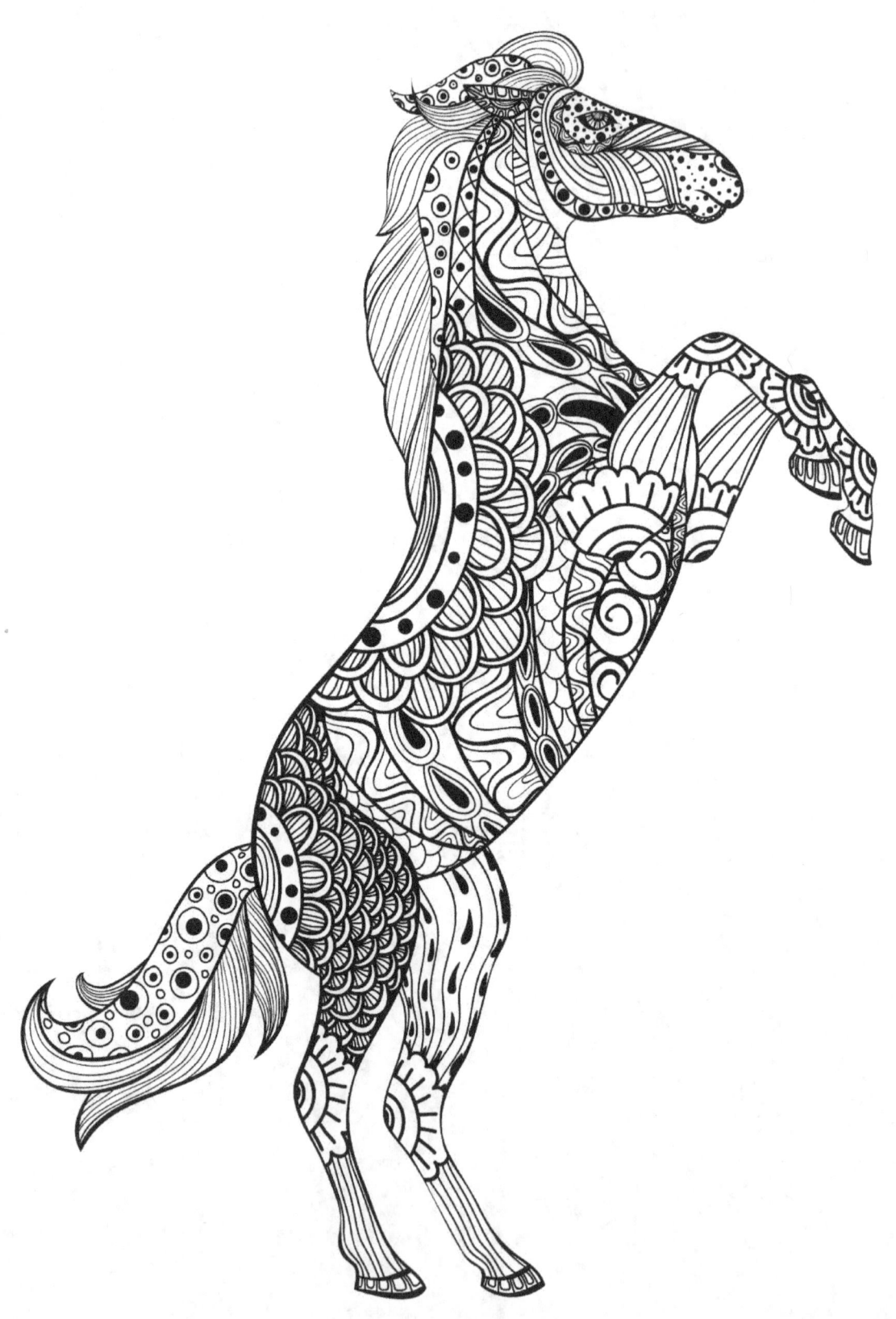

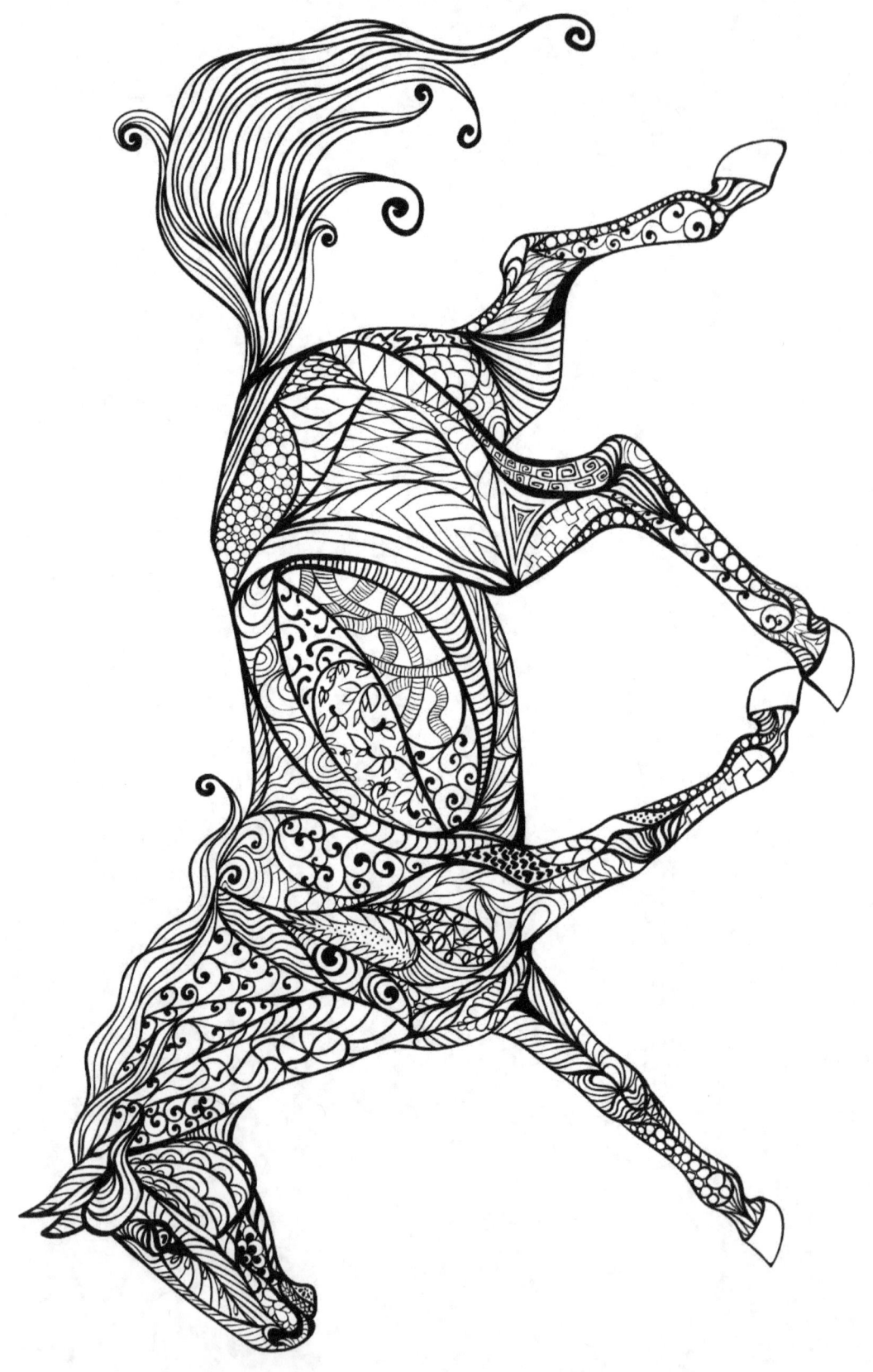

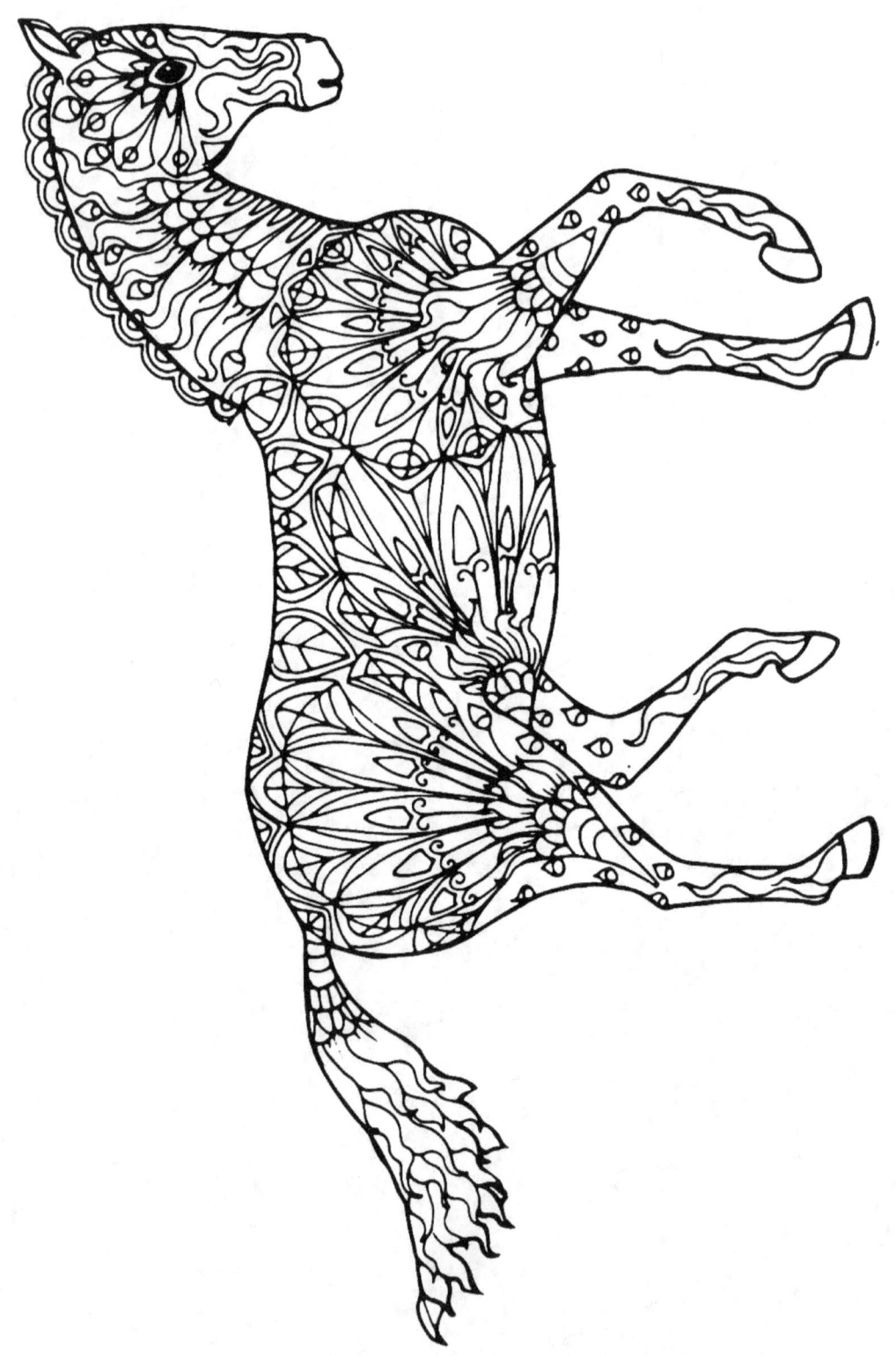

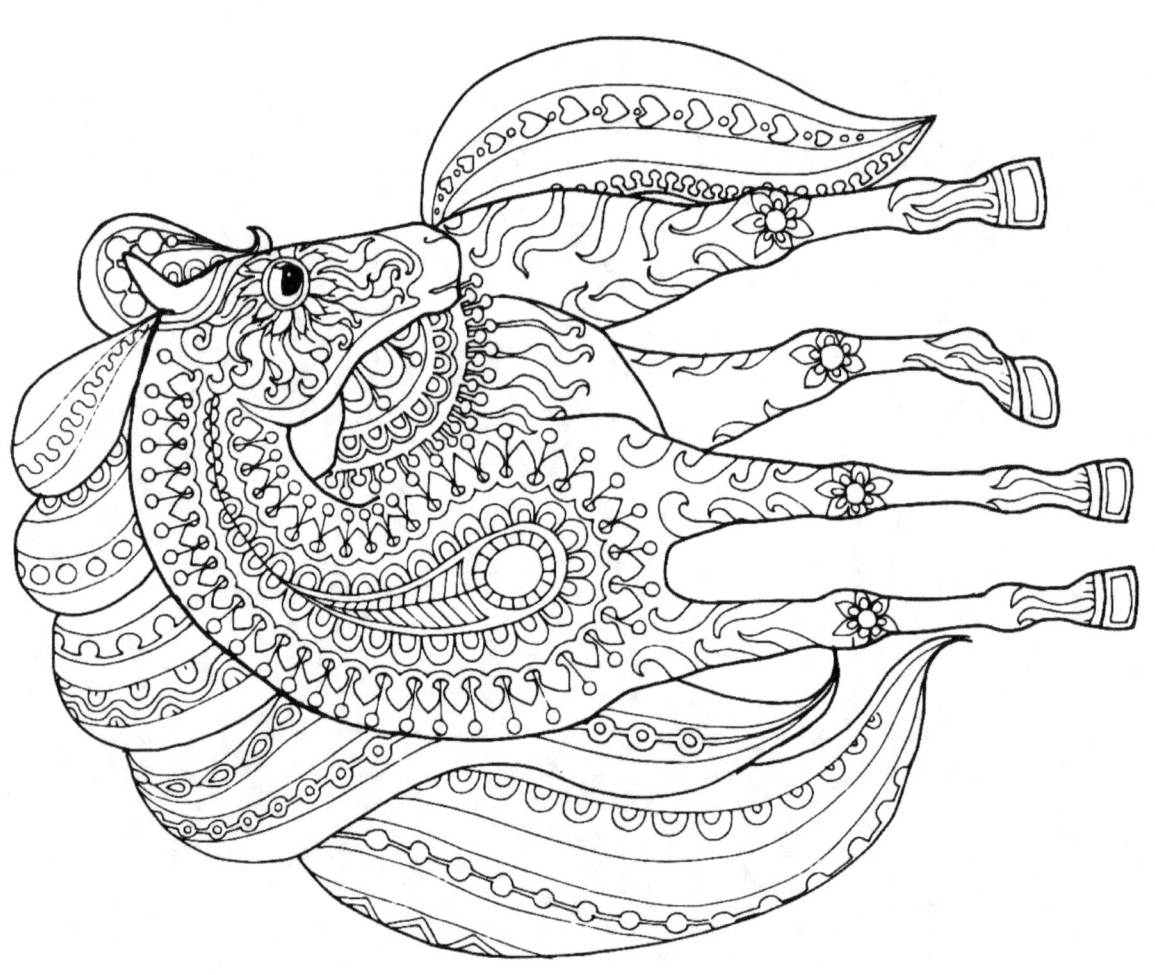

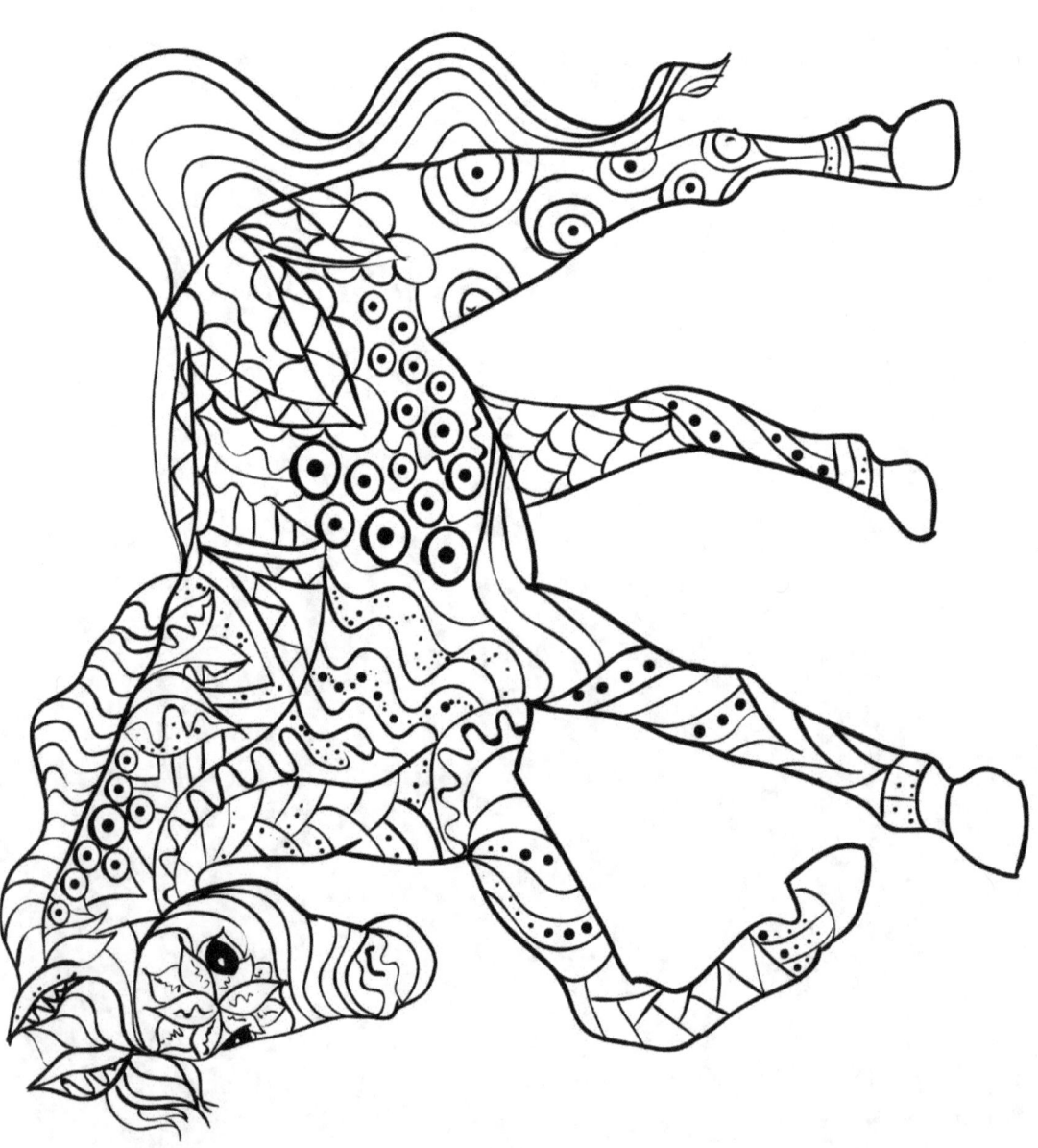

PDF Version this book : http://bit.ly/horses_c_2

Don't Miss Another our Books.

http://bit.ly/safari_coloring_b

ISBN : 9781523987931
(Use this ISBN for searching on amazon.com)

Join Us >> http://bit.ly/get_sample_free

- Get Free "Reviw Copies" of our New releases
- Exclusive offers and book giveaways
- More events from our community

Thank you

www.ingramcontent.com/pod-product-compliance
Lightning Source LLC
Chambersburg PA
CBHW081600280526
45788CB00011B/3529